Raising Children Compassionately

Parenting the Nonviolent
Communication^{SM} Way

*A presentation of Nonviolent
Communication^{SM} ideas and their use by*

Marshall B. Rosenberg, Ph.D.

PuddleDancer
P R E S S

P.O. Box 231129, Encinitas, CA 92023–1129
email@PuddleDancer.com • www.PuddleDancer.com

For additional information:
Center for Nonviolent Communication, 2428 Foothill Blvd., Suite E, La Crescenta, CA 91214
Tel: 818-957-9393 • Fax: 818-957-1424 • E-mail: cnvc@CNVC.org • Website: www.CNVC.org

Raising Children Compassionately:
Parenting the Nonviolent Communication Way

ISBN: 1-892005-09-3

Copyright © 2003 PuddleDancer Press

Author: Marshall B. Rosenberg, Ph.D.

Editor: Graham Van Dixhorn, Susan Kendrick Writing, kendrick@cheqnet.net

Cover and Interior Design: Lightbourne, www.lightbourne.com

Requests for permission should be addressed to:

PuddleDancer Press
Permissions Dept.
P.O. Box 231129
Encinitas, CA 92023-1129
Fax: 858-759-6967
email@PuddleDancer.com

Contents

Raising Children Compassionately

Introduction

I've been teaching Nonviolent Communication to parents for 30 years. I would like to share some of the things that have been helpful to both myself and to the parents that I've worked with, and to share with you some insights I've had into the wonderful and challenging occupation of parenting.

I'd first like to call your attention to the danger of the word "child," if we allow it to apply a different quality of respect than we would give to someone who is not labeled a child. Let me show you what I am referring to.

In parent workshops that I've done over the years, I've often started by dividing the group into two. I put one group in one room, and the other in a different room, and I give each group the task of writing down on a large paper a dialogue between themselves and another person in a conflict situation. I tell both groups what the conflict is. The only difference is that I tell one group the other person is their child, and to the second group I say the other person is their neighbor.

Then we get back into a large group and we look at these different sheets of paper outlining the dialogue that the groups would have, in the one case thinking that the other person was their child, and in the other case, the neighbor. (And incidentally, I haven't allowed the groups to discuss with the other group who the person was in their situation, so that both groups think that the situation is the same.)

After they've had a chance to scan the written dialogues of both groups, I ask them if they can see a difference in terms of the degree of respect and compassion that was demonstrated. Every time I've done this, the group that was working on the situation with the other person being a child was seen as being less respectful and compassionate in their communication than the group that saw the other person as a neighbor. This painfully reveals to the people in these groups how easy it is to dehumanize someone by the simple process of simply thinking of him or her as "our child."

My Own Awareness

I had an experience one day that really heightened my awareness of the danger of thinking of people as children. This experience followed a weekend in which I had worked with two groups: a street gang and a police department. I was mediating between the two groups. There had been considerable violence between them, and they had asked that I serve in the role of a mediator. After spending as much time as I did with them, dealing with the violence they had toward each other, I was exhausted. And as I was driving home afterwards, I told myself, I never want to be in the middle of another conflict for the rest of my life.

And of course, when I walked in my back door, my three children were fighting. I expressed my pain to them in a way that we advocate in Nonviolent Communication. I expressed how I was feeling, what my needs were, and what my requests were. I did it this way. I shouted, "When I hear all of this going on right now, I feel extremely tense! I have a real need for some peace and quiet after the weekend I've been through! So would you all be willing to give me that time and space?"

My oldest son looked at me and said, "Would you like to talk about it?" Now, at that moment, I dehumanized him in my thinking. Why? Because I said to myself, "How cute. Here's a nine year old boy trying to help his father." But take a closer look at how I was disregarding his offer because of his age, because I had him labeled as a child. Fortunately I saw that was going on in my head, and maybe I was able to see it more clearly because the work I had been doing between the street gang and the police showed me the danger of thinking of people in terms of labels instead of their humanness.

So instead of seeing him as a child and thinking to myself, "how cute," I saw a human being who was reaching out to another human being in pain, and I said out loud, "Yes, I would like to talk about it." And the three of them followed me into another room and listened while I opened up my heart to how painful it was to see that people could come to a point of wanting to hurt one another simply because they hadn't been trained to see the other person's humanness. After talking about it for 45 minutes I felt wonderful, and as I recall we turned the stereo on and danced like fools for awhile.

Our Education As Parents

So I'm not suggesting that we don't use words like "child" as a shorthand way of letting people know that we're talking about people of a certain age. I'm talking about when we allow labels like this to keep us from seeing the other person as a human being, in a way which leads us to dehumanize the other person because of the things our culture teaches us about "children." Let me show you an extension of what I'm talking about, how the label child can lead us to behave in a way that's quite unfortunate.

Having been educated, as I was, to think about parenting, I thought that it was the job of a parent to make children behave. You see, once you define yourself as an authority, a teacher or parent, in the culture that I was educated in, you then see it as your responsibility to make people that you label a "child" or a "student" behave in a certain way.

I now see what a self-defeating objective this is, because I have learned that any time it's our objective to get another person to behave in a certain way, people are likely to resist no matter what it is we're asking for. This seems to be true whether the other person is 2 or 92 years of age.

This objective of getting what we want from other people, or getting them to do what we want them to do, threatens the autonomy of people, their right to choose what they want to do. And whenever people feel that they're not free to choose what they want to do, they are likely to resist, even if they see the purpose in what we are asking and would ordinarily want to do it. So strong is our need to protect our autonomy, that if we see that someone has this single-mindedness of purpose, if they are acting like they think that they know what's best for us and are not leaving it to us to make the choice of how we behave, it stimulates our resistance.

The Limitations of Coercion and Punishment

I'll be forever grateful to my children for educating me about the limitations of the objective of getting other people to do what you want. They taught me that, first of all, I couldn't make them do what I want. I couldn't make them do anything. I couldn't make them put a toy back in the toy box. I couldn't make them make their bed. I couldn't make them eat. Now, that was quite a humbling lesson for me as a parent, to learn about my powerless-ness, because some-where I had gotten it into my mind that it was the job of a parent to make a child behave. And here were these young children teach-ing me this humbling lesson, that I couldn't make them do anything. All I could do is make them wish they had.

And whenever I would be foolish enough to do that, that is, to make them wish they had, they taught me a second lesson about parenting and power that has proven very valuable to me over the years. And that lesson was that anytime I would make them wish they had, they would make me wish I hadn't made them wish they had. Violence begets violence.

They taught me that any use of coercion on my part would invari-ably create resistance on their part, which could lead to an adversar-ial quality in the connection between us. I don't want to have that quality of connection with any human being, but especially not with my children, those human beings that I'm closest to and taking responsibility for. So my children are the last people that I want to get into these coercive games of which punishment is a part.

Now this concept of punishment is strongly advocated by most parents. Studies indicate that about 80% of American parents firm-ly believe in corporal punishment of children. This is about the same percentage of the population who believes in capital punishment of criminals. So with such a high percentage of the population believ-ing that punishment is justified and necessary in the education of children, I've had plenty of opportunity over the years to discuss this issue with parents, and I'm pleased with how people can be helped to see the limitations of any kind of punishment, if they'll simply ask themselves two questions.

Question number one: What do you want the child to do differently? If we ask only that question, it can certainly seem that punishment sometimes works, because certainly through the threat of punishment or application of punishment, we can at times influence a child to do what we would like the child to do.

However, when we add a second question, it has been my experience that parents see that punishment never works. The second question is: What do we want the child's reasons to be for acting as we would like them to act? It's that question that helps us to see that punishment not only doesn't work, but it gets in the way of our children doing things for reasons that we would like them to do them.

Since punishment is so frequently used and justified, parents can only imagine that the opposite of punishment is a kind of permissiveness in which we do nothing when children behave in ways that are not in harmony with our values. So therefore parents can think only, "If I don't punish, then I give up my own values and just allow the child to do whatever he or she wants." As I'll be discussing below, there are other approaches besides permissiveness, that is, just letting people do whatever they want to do, or coercive tactics such as punishment. And while I'm at it, I'd like to suggest that reward is just as coercive as punishment. In both cases we are using power *over* people, controlling the environment in a way that tries to force people to behave in ways that we like. In that respect reward comes out of the same mode of thinking as punishment.

A Certain Quality of Connection

There is another approach besides doing nothing or using coercive tactics. It requires an awareness of the subtle but important difference between our objective being to get people to do what we want, which I'm not advocating, and instead being clear that our objective is to create the quality of connection necessary for everyone's needs to get met.

It has been my experience, whether we are communicating with children or adults, that when we see the difference between these two objectives, and we are consciously not trying to get a person to do what we want, but trying to create a quality of mutual concern, a quality of mutual respect, a quality where both parties think that their needs matter and they are conscious that their needs and the other person's wellbeing are interdependent—it is amazing how conflicts which otherwise seem irresolvable, are easily resolved.

Now, this kind of communication that is involved in creating the quality of connection necessary for everybody's needs to get met is quite different from that communication used if we are using coercive forms of resolving differences with children. It requires a shift away from evaluating children in moralistic terms such as right/wrong, good/bad, to a language based on needs. We need to be able to tell children whether what they're doing is in harmony with our needs, or in conflict with our needs, but to do it in a way that doesn't stimulate guilt or shame on the child's part. So it might require our saying to the child, "I'm scared when I see you hitting your brother, because I have a need for people in the family to be safe," instead of, "It's wrong to hit your brother." Or it might require a shift away from saying, "You are lazy for not cleaning up your room," to saying, "I feel frustrated when I see that the bed isn't made, because I have a real need for support in keeping order in the house."

This shift in language away from classifying children's behavior in terms of right and wrong, and good and bad, to a language based on needs, is not easy for those of us who were educated by teachers and parents to think in moralistic judgments. It also requires an ability to be present to our children, and listen to them with empathy when they are in distress. This is not easy when we have been trained as parents to want to jump in and give advice, or to try to fix things.

So when I'm working with parents, we look at situations that are likely to arise where a child might say something like, "Nobody likes me." When a child says something like that, I believe the child needs an empathic kind of connection. And by that I mean a respectful understanding where the child feels that we are there and really hear what he or she is feeling and needing. Sometimes we can do this silently, just showing in our eyes that we are with their feelings of sadness, and their need for a different quality of connection with their friends. Or it could involve our saying out loud something like, "So it sounds like you're really feeling sad, because you aren't having very much fun with your friends."

But many parents, defining their role as requiring them to make their children happy all the time, jump in when a child says something like that, and say things like, "Well, have you looked at what you've been doing that might have been driving your friends away?" Or they disagree with the child, saying, "Well, that's not true. You've had friends in the past. I'm sure you'll get more friends." Or they give advice: "Maybe if you'd talk differently to your friends, your friends would like you more."

What they don't realize is that all human beings, when they're in pain, need presence and empathy. They may want advice, but they want that after they've received the empathic connection. My own children have taught me the hard way that, "Dad, please withhold all advice unless you receive a request in writing from us signed by a notary."

The Limitations of Rewards

Many people believe that it's more humane to use reward than punishment. But both of them I see as power *over* others, and Nonviolent Communication is based on power *with* people. And in power *with* people, we try to have influence not by how we can make people suffer if they don't do what we want, or how we can reward them if they do. It's a power based on mutual trust and respect, which makes people open to hearing each other and learning from each other, and to giving to one another willingly out of a desire to contribute to one another's wellbeing, rather than out of a fear of punishment or hope for a reward.

We get this kind of power, power *with* people, by being able to openly communicate our feelings and needs without in any way criticizing the other person. We do that by offering them what we would like from them in a way that is not heard as demanding or threatening. And as I have said, it also requires really hearing what other people are trying to communicate, showing an accurate understanding rather than quickly jumping in and giving advice, or trying to fix things.

For many parents, the way I'm talking about communicating is so different that they say, "Well, it just doesn't seem natural to communicate that way." At just the right time, I read something that Gandhi had written in which he said, "Don't mix up that which is habitual with that which is natural." Gandhi said that very often we've been trained to communicate and act in ways that are quite unnatural, but they are habitual in the sense that we have been trained for various reasons to do it that way in our culture. And that certainly rang true to me in the way that I was trained to communicate with children. The way I was trained to communicate by judging rightness and wrongness, goodness and badness, and the use of punishment was widely used and very easily became habitual for me as a parent. But I wouldn't say that because something is habitual that it is natural.

I learned that it is much more natural for people to connect in a loving, respectful way, and to do things out of joy for each other, rather than using punishment and reward or blame and guilt as means of coercion. But such a transformation does require a good deal of consciousness and effort.

Transforming Your Habitual Communication

I can recall one time when I was transforming myself from a habitually judgmental way of communicating with my children to the way that I am now advocating. On the day I'm thinking of, my oldest son and I were having a conflict, and it was taking me quite awhile to communicate it in the way that I was choosing to, rather than the way that had become habitual. Almost everything that came into my mind originally was some coercive statement in the form of a judgment of him for saying what he did. So I had to stop and take a deep breath, and think of how to get more in touch with my needs, and how to get more in touch with his needs. And this was taking me awhile. And he was getting frustrated because he had a friend waiting for him outside, and he said, "Daddy, it's taking you so long to talk." And I said, "Let me tell you what I can say quickly: Do it my way or I'll kick your butt." He said, "Take your time, Dad. Take your time."

So yes, I would rather take my time and come from an energy that I choose in communicating with my children, rather than habitually responding in a way that I have been trained to do, when it's not really in harmony with my own values. Sadly, we will often get much more reinforcement from those around us for behaving in a punitive, judgmental way, than in a way that is respectful to our children.

I can recall one Thanksgiving dinner when I was doing my best to communicate with my youngest son in the way that I am advocating, and it was not easy, because he was testing me to the limits. But I was taking my time, taking deep breaths, trying to understand what his needs were, trying to understand my own needs so I could express them in a respectful way. Another member of the family, observing my conversation with my son, but who had been trained in a different way of communicating, reached over at one point and whispered in my ear, "If that was my child, he'd be sorry for what he was saying."

I've talked to a lot of other parents who have had similar experiences who, when they are trying to relate in more human ways with their own children, instead of getting support, often get criticized. People can often mistake what I'm talking about as permissiveness or not giving children the direction they need, instead of understanding that it's a different quality of direction. It's a direction that comes from two parties trusting each other, rather than one party forcing his or her authority on another.

One of the most unfortunate results of making our objective to get our children to do what we want, rather than having our objective be for all of us to get what we want, is that eventually our children will be hearing a demand in whatever we are asking. And whenever people hear a demand, it's hard for them to keep focus on the value of whatever is being requested, because, as I said earlier, it threatens their autonomy, and that's a strong need that all people have. They want to be able to do something when they choose to do it, and not because they are forced to do it. As soon as a person hears a demand, it's going to make any resolution that will get everybody's needs met much harder to come by.

"Chore Wars"

For example, my children were given different tasks to do around the house. My youngest son, Brett, then 12, was being asked to take the garbage out, twice a week, so that it could be picked up by the garbage removal people. This involved a simple act of removing the garbage from underneath the kitchen sink, and taking it out on the front lawn where it could be picked up. This whole process could be done in 5 minutes. But it created a battle twice a week when the garbage was to go out.

Now, how did this battle start? It usually started with my simply mentioning his name. I would say, "Brett." But of course, the way I said it he could pick up that I was already angry because I was judging him as not doing what he should do. And even though I was saying his name loud enough so that the neighbors two blocks down could hear it, what does he do to keep escalating the war? He pretends that he doesn't hear me, even though he's in the next room. Well, what do I do? I get even angrier of course, and I escalate further, and now I say the name even louder the second time than the first time, so that even he can't pretend that he doesn't hear me. And what does he do? He says, "What do you want?" I say, "The garbage isn't out." He says, "You're very perceptive." And I say, "Get it out." And he says, "I will, later." And I say, "You said that last time but you didn't do it." And he says, "That doesn't mean I won't do it this time."

Look at all that energy going into the simple act of getting the garbage taken out. All the tension it creates between us, all because at that time I had it in my mind that it was his job to do it, that he should do it, that it was necessary for him to learn responsibility. So in other words, it was being presented to him as a demand.

People receive requests as demands if they think they will be punished or blamed if they don't do the task. When people have that idea, it takes all the joy out of doing anything.

One night I had a talk with Brett about this at a time when I was starting to get the point. I was starting to see how my thinking that I knew what was right, that my job as a parent was to get the children to behave, was destructive. So one night we had a talk about why the garbage wasn't going out, and by this time I was starting to learn how to listen better, to hear the feelings and needs that were behind his not doing what I asked. And I saw so clearly that he had a need to do things because he chose to do them, and not to do them simply because he was being forced to do them.

So when I saw this, I said to him, Brett, how do we get out of this? I know I really have been making demands in the past in the sense that when you didn't do things I wanted you to do, I would make judgments of you as being not a cooperative member of the family. So how do we get out of this history that we have, and how do we get to a place where we can do things for one another out of a different kind of energy? And he came up with an idea that was very helpful. He said, "Dad, how about if I'm not sure if it's a request or a demand, I ask you, 'Is that a request or a demand?'" I said, "Hey, I like that idea. It would force me to really stop and look at my thinking, and really see whether I am actually saying, 'Hey, I'd really like you to do this, it would meet my need, but if your needs are in conflict I'd like to hear that, and let's figure out a way to get everybody's needs met.'"

I liked his suggestion, to stop and really see what kind of assumptions were going on in me. And the next day, before he went to school, we had three chances to test this out. Because three times in the morning I asked him to do something, and each time he looked at me and said, "Dad, is that a request or a demand?" And each time I looked inside, I saw that it was still a demand. I still had this thinking in me that he should do it, that it was the only reasonable thing for him to do. I was prepared that if he didn't do it, to get progressively more coercive. So it was helpful that he called this to my attention. Each time I stopped, got in touch with my needs, tried to hear his needs, and I said to him, "Okay, thank you. That helps. It was a demand, and now it's a request." And he could sense the difference in me. And each of those three times he did it without question.

When people hear demands, it looks to them as though our caring and respect and love are conditional. It looks as though we are only going to care for them as people when they do what we want.

Unconditional Love

I remember one time, years ago, when Brett was 3 years old. I was wondering if I was communicating an unconditional quality of love to him and my other children as well. But he happened to be the one that came upon me at that time when I was thinking about this subject. As he came into the living room I said, "Brett, why does Dad love you?" He looked at me and immediately said, "Because I make my potties in the toilet now?" I felt very sad the moment he said that because it was so clear, how could he think differently? How differently I respond to my children when they do what I want, than when they don't do what I want.

So I said to him, "Well, I do appreciate that, but that's not why I love you." And then he said, "Well, because I don't throw my food on the floor anymore?" He was referring there to a little disagreement we'd had the night before when he was throwing some food on the floor. And I said, "Well, here again, I do appreciate it when you keep your food on your plate. But that's not why I love you."

Now he gets very serious, and looks at me and says, "Well, why do you love me, Daddy?" And now I was wondering, why did I get into abstract conversation about unconditional love with a 3 year old? How do you express this to someone his age? And I blurted out, "Well, I just love you because you're you." At the time, the immediate thought I had was, that's pretty trite and vague, but he got it. He got the message. I just saw it in his face. He brightened up and he looked at me and he said, "Oh, you just love me because I'm me, Daddy. You just love me because I'm me." The next two days it seemed like every ten minutes he was running over to me and pulling at my side and looking up and saying, "You just love me because I'm me, Daddy. You just love me because I'm me."

So to communicate this quality of unconditional love, respect, acceptance to other people, this doesn't mean that we have to like what they're doing. It doesn't mean we have to be permissive and give up our needs or values. What it requires is that we show people the same quality of respect when they don't do what we ask, as when they do. After we have shown that quality of respect through empathy, through taking the time to understand why they didn't do what we would like, we can then pursue how we might influence them to willingly do what we ask. In some cases, where people are behaving in a serious way that threatens our needs or safety and there's not time or ability to communicate about it, we may even use force.

But unconditional love requires that no matter how people behave, they trust that they'll receive a certain quality of understanding from us.

Preparing Our Children

Now of course, our children are often going to be in situations where they're not going to receive this unconditional acceptance and respect and love. They're going to be in schools, perhaps, where the teachers are using a form of authority that's based on other ways of thinking, namely that you have to earn respect and love—that you deserve to be punished or blamed if you don't behave in a certain way. So one of our tasks as parents is to show our children a way of staying human, even when they are being exposed to others who are using a form of coercion.

One of my happiest days as a parent was when my oldest son went off to a neighborhood school. He was 12 years old at the time. He had just finished 6 years in a school where I'd helped train the teachers, a school based on principles of Nonviolent Communication where people were expected to do things not because of punishment or reward, but because they saw how it was contributing to their own and other people's wellbeing, where evaluation was in terms of needs and requests, not in terms of judgments. So this was going to be quite a different experience for him after six years in such a school, to go to the neighborhood school, which I'm sad to say wasn't functioning in a way that I would have liked.

But before he had gone off to this school, I had tried to provide him with some understanding of why teachers in this school might be communicating and behaving in a different way, and I tried to provide him with some skills for handling that situation should it occur. When he came home from school the first day I was delighted to find out how he had used what I had offered him.

I asked him, "Rick, how was the new school?" And he said, "Oh, it's okay, Dad. But boy, some of those teachers." I could see that he was distressed, and I said, "What happened?"

He said, "Dad, I wasn't even halfway in the door, really I was just walking in, when this man teacher saw me and came running over and screamed at me, 'My, my, look at the little girl.'" Now, what that teacher was reacting to was, my son had long hair at the time, down to his shoulders. And this teacher had a way of thinking, apparently, where he thought he as the authority knew what was right, that there was a right way to wear hair, and that if somebody doesn't do things the right way, then you have to shame them or guilt them or punish them into doing it.

I felt sad to hear that my child would be greeted that way his first moment in the new school. And I said, "How did you handle it?" And he said, "Dad, I remembered what you said, that when you're in a place like that, never to give them the power to make you submit or rebel." Well, I was delighted that he would remember that abstract principle at such a time. And I told him I was glad that he remembered it, and I said, "How did you handle the situation?"

He said, "Dad, I also did what you suggested, that when people are talking to me that way, to try to hear what they're feeling and needing and not take it personally. Just to try to hear their feelings and needs." I said, "Wow, am I glad that you thought to do that. What did you hear?"

He said, "Dad, it was pretty obvious. I heard that he was irritated and wanted me to cut my hair." "Oh," I said, "how did that leave you feeling, to receive his message in that way?" And he said, "Dad, I felt really sad for the man. He was bald, and seemed to have a problem about hair."

The "Captain" Game

I had a very good experience with my children when they were 3, 4 and 7 years old. I was then writing a book for teachers about how to create schools in harmony with principles of Nonviolent Communication, in harmony with principles of mutual respect between teachers and students, schools that fostered the values of autonomy and interdependence. And as part of the research I was doing in setting up these schools, I was wanting to learn more about what kind of choices we could trust children to make. And to be able to turn these decisions over to children so that they were better able to develop their ability to make choices in their lives.

At this time, I thought a good way of learning more about this might be to play a game with my children which we called Captain. In this game each day I would appoint one of the children as Captain. And when it was their turn as the Captain, I would turn over many decisions that I would usually make, to the Captain to make. But I wouldn't give this decision to the child unless I was prepared to live with however they made the choice. As I said, my purpose in this game was to learn how children could make choices, how early they could make certain choices, and which ones might not be easy for them to make.

Here is an example of how this game went, and what a good learning experience it was for me. Once I took the children with me to pick up some dry cleaning, and as I paid, the woman started to hand me three pieces of candy for the children. Immediately I saw a good opportunity to turn a decision over to the Captain. As the woman handed me the candy, I said, "Uh, would you please give the candy to the Captain?"

Well, she didn't know what I was talking about, but the Captain did. Three-year-old Brett walked over, held out his hand, and she placed the candy in his hand. And then I said, "Captain, would you please choose what to do with this candy?"

Well, now imagine this rough decision for this 3 year old Captain. Here he is, 3 pieces of candy in his hand, he has a sister looking at him, he has a brother looking at him, how does he choose? Well, after a serious consideration, he gave one piece to his brother, and one piece to his sister, and he ate the other himself.

When I first told that story to a group of parents, one of the parents said, "Well, yes, but that's because you had taught him that it was right to share." And I said to the parent, "Oh, not accurate. I know that's not so, because a week before he was in a very similar situation, and he ate all 3 pieces of candy. Can you guess what happened to him the next day? Yes, he learned the next day that if we don't take other people's needs into consideration, that our own needs can never really be met. He really got a quick lesson on interdependence. It was thrilling for me to see how quickly children saw this when they really had choices to make. That we can never really take care of ourselves without showing equal concern for the needs of others."

As I said earlier, it's not easy for parents to let go of the concept of punishment. It's deeply ingrained in many parents that this is a necessity. And they can't imagine what else can be done when children are behaving in ways that might be harmful to themselves and other people. And they can't conceive of other options besides permissiveness, just letting it go, or using some kind of punitive action.

The Use of Force

I have found it very important to get across to such parents the concept of the protective use of force, and to get them to see the difference between the protective use of force and the punitive use of force. So when might we sometimes have to use a form of force with our children?

Well, the conditions calling for this would be when there isn't time to communicate, and the child's behavior might be injurious to themselves or other people. Or it could be that the person isn't willing to talk. So if a person isn't willing to talk, or there isn't time to talk, and meanwhile they are behaving in a way that is conflict with one of our needs, such as a need to protect people, we might have to use force. But now we have to see the difference between the protective and the punitive use of force. And one way that these two uses of force differ is in the thinking of the person who is engaging in the force.

In the punitive use of force, the person using such force has made a moralistic judgment of the other person, a judgment that implies some kind of wrongness that is deserving of punishment. This person deserves to suffer for what they've done. That's the whole idea of punishment. It comes out of these ideas that human beings are basically sinful, evil creatures and the corrective process is to make them penitent. We have to get them to see how terrible they are for doing what they're doing. And the way we make them penitent is to use some form of punishment to make them suffer. Sometimes this can be a physical punishment in the form of spanking, or it could be a psychological punishment in the form of trying to make them hate themselves, through making them feel guilty or ashamed.

The thinking behind the protective use of force is radically different. There is no consciousness that the other person is bad or deserving of punishment. Our consciousness is fully focused on our needs. We are conscious of what need of ours is in danger. But we are not in any way implying badness or wrongness to the child.

So this kind of thinking is one significant difference between the protective use of force and the punitive use of force. And this thinking is closely related to a second difference, the intent. In the punitive use of force, it is our intent to create pain and suffering for the other person, to make them sorry for what they did. In the protective use of force, our intent is only to protect. We protect our needs and then later we'll have the communication necessary to educate the person. But at the moment it may be necessary to use the force to protect.

An example of this would be, when my children were young, we lived on a busy street. And they seemed to be fascinated with what was going on across the street, and they hadn't yet learned the dangers of what can happen to you if you just dart out in the street. I was certain that if we could talk long enough about this, I could educate them, but in the meantime I was afraid that they could be killed. So here was a case for the protective use of force, there not being the time to communicate about this before something serious could happen. So what I said to them was, "If I see you running in the street, I'm going to put you in the back yard where I don't have to worry about you getting hit by a car." Not long after I said that, one of them forgot and started to run in the street. I picked him up, carried him into the yard and put him there, not as a punishment, there was plenty to do in the yard, we had swings and a slide. I wasn't trying to make him suffer. I was only wanting to control the environment to meet my need for safety.

Now many parents say, "Well, isn't the child likely to see that as a punishment?" Well, if it has been intended as a punishment in the past, if the child has had a lot of experience seeing people as punitive, yes, they could still see it as a punishment. The main thing, though, is that we, the parents, are conscious of this difference, and that if we use force we're certain that it is to protect and not to punish.

One way of remembering the purpose of the protective use of force, is to see the difference between controlling the child, and controlling the environment. In punishment we're trying to control the child by making the child feel bad about what they've done, to create an internal shame, guilt or fear for what they have done.

In the protective use of force, our intent is not to control the child; it's to control the environment. To protect our needs until such time as we can have the quality of communication with the other person that's really necessary. It's somewhat like putting screens on our house to protect us from being bitten by mosquitoes. It's a protective use of force. We control the environment to prevent things happening that we don't want to happen.

Supportive Communities

Now the way of parenting that I'm advocating here is quite different from how most people are parenting. And it's going to be difficult to consider radically different options in a world where punishment is so prevalent, and where you are likely to be misinterpreted if you don't use punishment and other coercive forms of parental behavior. It really helps people immensely if they are part of a supportive community that understands the concept of parenting I'm talking about, where they have the support to continue to do this in a world that doesn't often support it.

I know that I was always much better able to stay with what I'm now talking about if I was getting a lot of empathy myself from a supportive community, empathy for how hard it can be to be a parent at times. How easy it is to fall into old patterns. When I had other parents similarly trying to connect with their children as I was, it was very supportive to be able to talk to them, and to hear their frustrations, to have them hear mine. And I noticed that the more that I was part of such a community; the better able I was to stay with this process with my children, even under difficult conditions.

And one of the rewarding things that happened that was very encouraging and enriching, was a message I received from my daughter when she was very small. It was on a Sunday morning, the only time of the week when I could relax, a very precious time for me.

Now, on this particular Sunday morning, a couple called me up and asked if I would be willing to see them in counseling. They had a crisis in their relationship, and wanted me to work with them. And I agreed to do this without really looking inside myself and seeing what my own needs were, and how I was resenting their intrusion on my time to relax. While I had them in the living room counseling them, the doorbell rang and the police were bringing in a young woman for me to see. I had also been seeing her in counseling, and they had found her down on the railroad tracks. That was her way of letting me know she wanted to see me. She was too shy to call up and ask for another appointment. This was her way, sitting on the railroad tracks, of letting me know she was in distress. She knew the train schedule better than anyone in town, so she knew the police would pick her up before the train got her.

So then the police left, and I had this young woman in the kitchen crying, and the couple in the living room, and I was going back and forth trying to lovingly counsel both. And while I was doing this, walking from one room to the other, looking at my watch, hoping I would still have time afterwards to have some time to myself, the three children upstairs started fighting. So I bounded up the stairs, and I found something fascinating. I might write this up in a scientific paper some day: the effect of altitude on maniac behavior. Because you see, downstairs I was a very loving person, giving love to this couple, giving love to the young woman in the other room, but one flight of stairs up and I was a maniac.

I said to my children, "What's the matter with you? Can't you see that I have hurting people downstairs? Now get in your rooms!" And each went in their rooms and slammed the door just loud enough that I couldn't prove it was a slam, and when it happened the first time I got more outraged, and the second time even more. But fortunately the third time it happened, I don't know why, but it helped me see the humor in the situation. How easy it was for me to be loving of these people downstairs, but how quickly I could get brutal with my own family upstairs.

I took a deep breath and I went first in my oldest son's room and told him I was sad that I was taking out some feelings on him that I was afraid I really had in relation to the people downstairs. He understood, he just said, "It's okay, Dad. Nothing big." I went in my youngest son's room and got a pretty similar response from him. And when I went in my daughter's room and told her that I felt sad at the way I had talked to her, she came over and put her head on my shoulder and said, "It's okay, Daddy. Nobody's perfect."

What a precious message to hear. Yes, my children appreciate my efforts to relate to them in a caring way, in a compassionate way, an empathic way. But how relieving it is that they can understand my humanness and how difficult it can sometimes be.

So in closing I offer you that reassuring advice given to me by my daughter, that nobody's perfect, to remember that anything that's worth doing is worth doing poorly. And the job of parenting, of course, is extremely worth doing, but we're going to do it poorly at times. If we're going to be brutal with ourselves when we're not perfect parents, our children are going to suffer for that.

I often tell the parents that I'm working with that hell is having children and thinking there's such a thing as a good parent. That if every time we're less than perfect, we're going to blame ourselves and attack ourselves, our children are not going to benefit from that. So the goal I would suggest is not to be perfect parents, it's to become progressively less stupid parents — by learning from each time that we're not able to give our children the quality of understanding that they need, that we're not able to express ourselves honestly. In my experience, each of these times usually means that we're not getting the emotional support we need as parents, in order to give our children what they need.

We can only really give in a loving way to the degree that we are receiving similar love and understanding. So that's why I strongly recommend that we look at how we might create a supportive community for ourselves among our friends and others, who can give us the understanding we need to be present to our children in a way that will be good for them and good for us.

I hope that something I've said here has helped you grow closer to becoming the parent you would like to be.

Some Basic Feelings We All Have

Feelings when needs "are" fulfilled

• Amazed	• Joyous	• Comfortable	• Moved
• Confident	• Optimistic	• Eager	• Proud
• Energetic	• Relieved	• Fulfilled	• Stimulated
• Glad	• Surprised	• Hopeful	• Thankful
• Inspired	• Touched	• Intrigued	• Trustful

Feelings when needs "are not" fulfilled

• Angry	• Hopeless	• Annoyed	• Impatient
• Confused	• Irritated	• Concerned	• Lonely
• Disappointed	• Nervous	• Discouraged	• Overwhelmed
• Distressed	• Puzzled	• Embarrassed	• Reluctant
• Frustrated	• Sad	• Helpless	• Uncomfortable

Some Basic Needs We All Have

Autonomy
- Choosing dreams/goals/values
- Choosing plans for fulfilling one's dreams, goals, values

Celebration
- Celebrate the creation of life and dreams fulfilled
- Celebrate losses: loved ones, dreams, etc. (mourning)

Integrity
- Authenticity • Creativity
- Meaning • Self-worth

Interdependence
- Acceptance • Appreciation
- Closeness • Community
- Consideration
- Contribute to the enrichment of life
- Emotional Safety • Empathy

Physical Nurturance
- Air • Food
- Movement, exercise
- Protection from life-threatening forms of life: viruses, bacteria, insects, predatory animals
- Rest • Sexual expression
- Shelter • Touch • Water

Play
- Fun • Laughter

Spiritual Communion
- Beauty • Harmony
- Inspiration • Order • Peace

- Honesty (the empowering honesty that enables us to learn from our limitations)
- Love • Reassurance
- Respect • Support
- Trust • Understanding

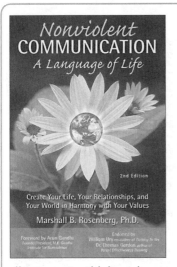

Nonviolent Communication^{SM}

A Language of Life, 2nd Edition

Marshall B. Rosenberg, Ph.D.

ISBN: 1-892005-03-4
Trade Paper 6x9 • Price: $17.95 US
Distributed by IPG: 800-888-4741

*Enjoy Powerful and Satisfying
Relationships . . . in All Areas of Your Life*

Most of us have been educated from birth to compete, judge, demand, diagnose—to think and communicate in terms of what is "right" and "wrong" with people. Even when we are well-meaning this can be disastrous to our relationships—both personal and professional. At best, the habitual ways we think and speak hinder communication, and create misunderstanding and frustration in others and in ourselves. And still worse, they cause anger and pain, and may lead to violence. Without wanting to, even people with the best of intentions generate needless conflict.

Nonviolent Communication helps you:

- Free yourself from the effects of past experiences and cultural conditioning
- Break patterns of thinking that lead to arguments, anger and depression
- Resolve conflicts peacefully, whether personal or public, domestic or international
- Create social structures that support everyone's needs being met
- Develop relationships based upon mutual respect, compassion, and cooperation

"Nonviolent communication is a simple yet powerful methodology for communicating in a way that meets both parties' needs. This is one of the most useful books you will ever read."
—WILLIAM URY, co-author of *Getting to Yes* and author of *The Third Side*

"This book gives people both a way of expressing their needs nonblamefully and a way of listening so others feel not just heard, but understood."
—DR. THOMAS GORDON, author, *Parent Effectiveness Training (P.E.T.)*

Available from CNVC, all major bookstores and Amazon.com
Distributed by IPG: 800-888-4741

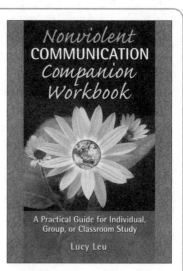

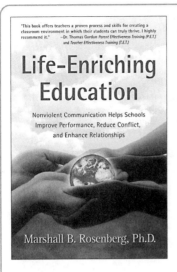

Additional NVC Books from PuddleDancer Press

We Can Work It Out $5.95
Resolving Conflicts Peacefully and Powerfully   (6x9, 32 pages)
by Marshall B. Rosenberg, Ph.D. • Practical suggestions for fostering
caring, genuine cooperation, and satisfying resolutions in even the most difficult
situations. ISBN: 1-892005-12-3

Raising Children Compassionately $5.95
Parenting the Nonviolent Communication Way   (6x9, 32 pages)
by Marshall B. Rosenberg, Ph.D. • This booklet, filled with insights
and stories, will prove invaluable for parents, teachers and others who want
to nurture children and also themselves. ISBN: 1-892005-09-3

Teaching Children Compassionately $7.95
How Students and Teachers Can Succeed with Mutual   (6x9, 48 pages)
Understanding • by Marshall B. Rosenberg, Ph.D.
Skills for creating a successful classroom—from a keynote address and workshop
given to a national conference of Montessori educators. ISBN: 1-892005-11-5

What's Making You Angry? $5.95
10 Steps to Transforming Anger So Everyone Wins   (6x9, 32 pages)
by Shari Klein and Neill Gibson • A step-by-step guide to re-focus your
attention when you're angry, and create outcomes that are satisfying for everyone.
ISBN: 1-892005-13-1

The Heart of Social Change $7.95
How to Make a Difference in Your World   (6x9, 48 pages)
by Marshall B. Rosenberg, Ph.D. • Marshall offers an insightful
perspective on effective social change, and how-to examples. ISBN: 1-892005-10-7

Parenting From Your Heart $7.95
Sharing the Gifts of Compassion, Connection, and Choice   (6x9, 48 pages)
by Inbal Kashtan • Addresses the challenges of parenting with real-world solutions
for creating family relationships that meet everyone's needs. ISBN: 1-892005-08-5

Getting Past the Pain Between Us $7.95
Healing and Reconciliation Without Compromise   (6x9, 48 pages)
by Marshall B. Rosenberg, Ph.D. • Learn the healing power of listening
and speaking from the heart. Skills for resolving conflicts, healing old hurts, and
reconciling strained relationships. ISBN: 1-892005-07-7

Available from CNVC, all major bookstores and Amazon.com. Distributed by IPG: 800-888-4741
For more information about these booklets visit www.NonviolentCommunication.com

NONVIOLENT COMMUNICATION MATERIALS

Available from CNVC at www.CNVC.org or call 800-255-7696

The Compassionate Classroom $18
Relationship Based Teaching and Learning   (7.5x9, 187 pages)
by **Sura Hart and Victoria Kindle Hodson, M.A.** • This new book provides
an overview of the NVC process and its relationship to successful teaching and learning,
and specific examples of how NVC can be used in elementary school classrooms includes
playful exercises, lesson plans, and skill-building activities and games.

The Giraffe Classroom $18
by **Nancy Sokol Green** • Humorous, creative, and   (8.5x11, spiral bound, 122 pages)
thought provoking activities. Ideal for teachers, parents, and anyone who wants to use
concrete exercises to learn the process of NVC.

Communication Basics $4
An Overview of Nonviolent Communication   (24 pages)
by **Rachelle Lamb** • This new booklet provides a clear, concise, and handy summary
of what one might learn in an introductory training in Nonviolent Communication.

Speaking Peace • by **Marshall B. Rosenberg, Ph.D.** .... 2 CD set: $25
This recording, produced by Sounds True, explains the purpose .... **2 Audio set: $20**
of NVC, how to use the 4 components of the NVC model to express ourselves   (2.5 hrs.)
honestly and respond empathically to others, and to bring about change within
ourselves, others, and within larger social systems; includes songs, stories and examples.

The Basics of Nonviolent Communication $50
An Introductory Training   (2 videotapes, 3 hrs)
by **Marshall B. Rosenberg, Ph.D.** • This edited one-day training shows how we
can connect with others in a way that enables everyone's needs to be met through
natural giving.

Making Life Wonderful $145
An Intermediate Training   (4 videotapes, over 8 hours)
by **Marshall B. Rosenberg, Ph.D.** • Improve relationships with self and others by
increasing fluency in NVC. Two-day training session in San Francisco filled with insights,
examples, extended role-plays, stories, and songs that will deepen your grasp of NVC.

THESE AND ADDITIONAL MATERIALS AVAILABLE AT:
(10% Member Discount available—Prices may change.)

Mail: CNVC, 2428 Foothill Blvd., Suite E, La Crescenta, CA 91214

Phone: 800-255-7696 (toll free order line) or by **Fax:** 1-818-957-1424

Shipping: First item $5.00, each additional $1.00 (For orders shipped outside
the United States, call 1-818-957-9393 to determine actual shipping charges.
Please pay with US dollars only.

Contributions And Membership: A contribution of $35 or more qualifies you
as a member of CNVC and entitles you to a 10% discount on CNVC materials
ordered from the Center. Your tax-deductible contribution of any amount will
be gratefully received and will help support CNVC projects worldwide.

2428 Foothill Blvd., Suite E, La Crescenta, CA 91214
Tel: (818) 957-9393 • Fax: (818) 957-1424
Email: cnvc@cnvc.org • Website: www.cnvc.org

The **Center for Nonviolent Communication** is a global organization whose vision is a world where everyone's needs are met peacefully. Our mission is to contribute to this vision by facilitating the creation of life-enriching systems within ourselves, inter-personally, and within organizations. We do this by living and teaching the process of Nonviolent Communication[SM] (NVC), which strengthens people's ability to compassionately connect with themselves and one another, share resources, and resolve conflicts peacefully.

CNVC is dedicated to fostering a compassionate response to people by honoring our universally shared needs for autonomy, celebration, integrity, interdependence, physical nurturance, play, and spiritual communion. We are committed to functioning, at every level of our organization and in all of our interactions, in harmony with the process we teach, operating by consensus, using NVC to resolve conflicts, and providing NVC training for our staff. We often work collaboratively with other organizations for a peaceful, just and ecologically balanced world.

Purpose, Mission, History, and Projects

For many years the Center for Nonviolent Communication has been showing people how to connect in ways that inspire compassionate results. We are now seeking funds to support projects in North America, Latin America, South America, Europe, Africa, South Asia, Brazil, and the Middle East, and to support our innovative projects for educators, parents, social change, and prison work.

A list of CNVC certified trainers and contact information for them may be found on the Center's website. This list is updated monthly. The website also includes information about CNVC sponsored trainings and links to affiliated regional websites. CNVC invites you to consider bringing NVC training to your business, school, church, or community group. For current information about trainings scheduled in your area, or if you would like to organize NVC trainings, be on the CNVC mailing list or support our efforts to create a more peaceful world, please contact CNVC.